Seymour Simon

SKYSCRAPERS

SeaStar Books • San Francisco

To Jeremy and Chloe

Permission to use the following photographs is gratefully acknowledged:

Front cover: © Stefano Amanti/Bruce Coleman Inc.; title page, page 4: © Massimo Borchi/Bruce Coleman Inc.; pages 2-3: © Comstock.com; pages 6-7: © Paul A. Souders/CORBIS; page 9: courtesy of Chicago Historical Society; page 10: © Comstock.com; pages 12-13: © Sami Sarkis/Getty Images; pages 14-15: © Walter Hodges/CORBIS; page 17: © Charles E. Rotkin/CORBIS; page 19: © Steven Dunwell/Getty Images; pages 20-21: © Stuart McCall/Getty Images; pages 22-23: © Joel Rogers/Getty Images; pages 24-25: © James Leynse/CORBIS; page 26: © Lee Foster/Bruce Coleman Inc.; page 29: © Glenn Short/Bruce Coleman Inc.; pages 30-31: © Guy Tillim/CORBIS SYGMA; page 32: © Comstock.com; back cover: © Comstock.com

Book design by E. Friedman.
Typeset in 18 ITC Century Book.
Manufactured in China.

SeaStar is an imprint of Chronicle Books LLC.

Library of Congress Cataloging-in-Publication Data
Simon, Seymour.
Skyscrapers / Seymour Simon.
p. cm.—(SeeMore readers)
Includes bibliographical references and index.
ISBN 1-58717-266-6 (library binding)
ISBN 1-58717-259-3 (pbk)
1. Skyscrapers—Juvenile literature. 2. Architecture, Modern—20th century—Juvenile literature. I. Title.
NA6230.S44 2005
720'.483—dc22
2004011331

Distributed in Canada by Raincoast Books
9050 Shaughnessy Street, Vancouver, British Columbia V6P 6E5

10 9 8 7 6 5 4 3 2 1

Chronicle Books LLC
85 Second Street, San Francisco, California 94105

www.chroniclekids.com

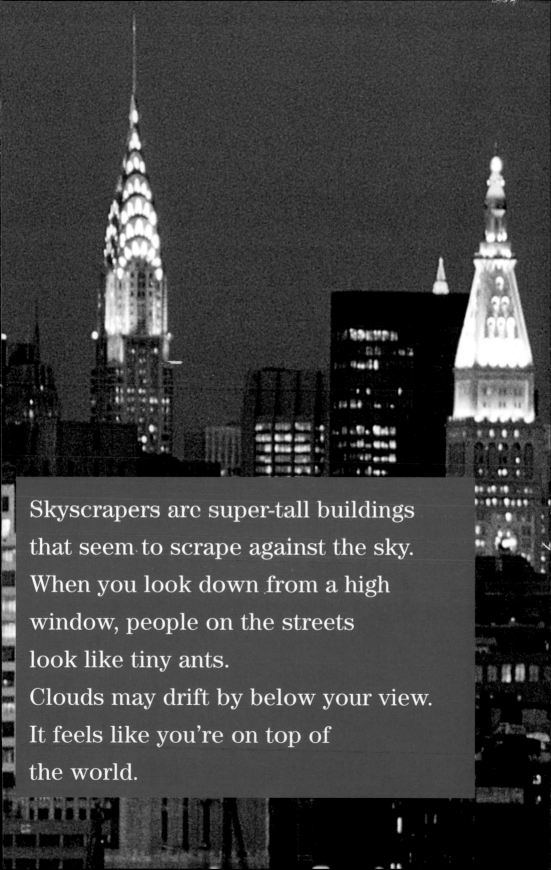

Skyscrapers are super-tall buildings
that seem to scrape against the sky.
When you look down from a high
window, people on the streets
look like tiny ants.
Clouds may drift by below your view.
It feels like you're on top of
the world.

Someday, new skyscrapers will be
built that reach even higher into
the sky.
No one knows how high we can go.

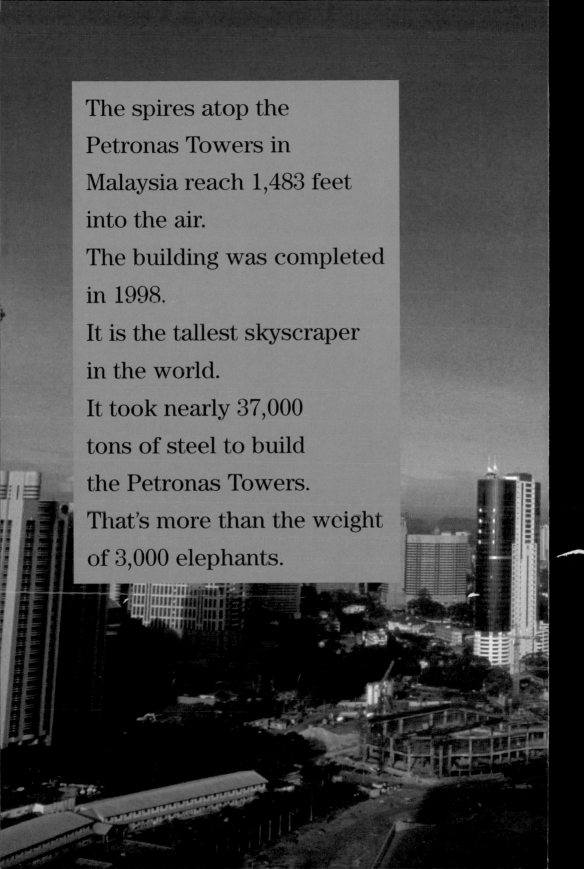

The spires atop the Petronas Towers in Malaysia reach 1,483 feet into the air.

The building was completed in 1998.

It is the tallest skyscraper in the world.

It took nearly 37,000 tons of steel to build the Petronas Towers.

That's more than the weight of 3,000 elephants.

The Sears Tower in Chicago is 1,450 feet tall and has 110 floors.

It is about as tall as five football fields laid end to end.

When it was finished in 1973, it was the world's tallest building.

It is still the tallest building in North America.

The Transamerica Pyramid in
San Francisco is 853 feet tall.
It is the only skyscraper in the world
built in the shape of a pyramid.
Three hundred miles of steel rods
were used to construct the
Transamerica Pyramid.
It takes a month to wash its
3,678 windows.

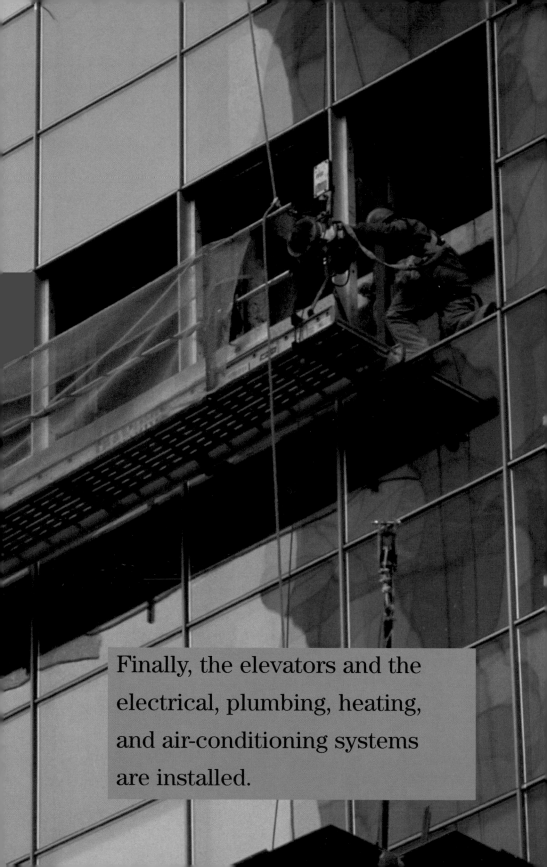

Finally, the elevators and the electrical, plumbing, heating, and air-conditioning systems are installed.

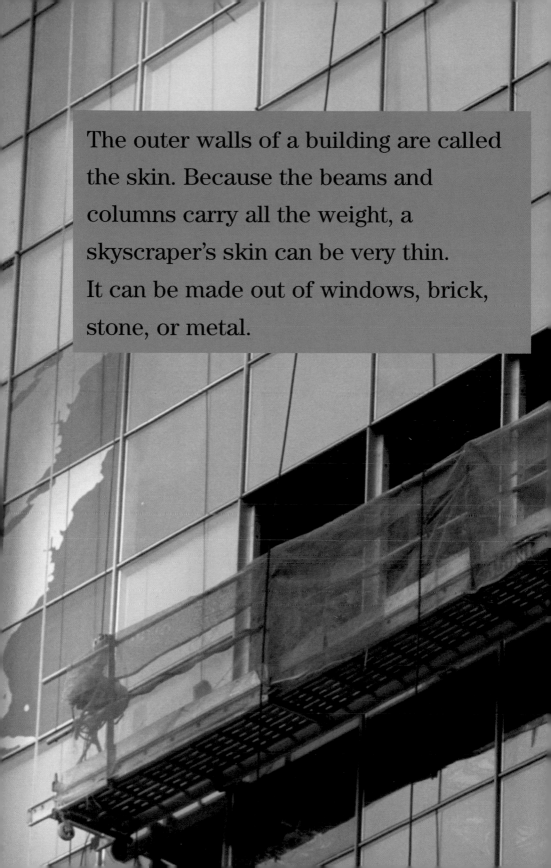

The outer walls of a building are called the skin. Because the beams and columns carry all the weight, a skyscraper's skin can be very thin. It can be made out of windows, brick, stone, or metal.

Floors help keep the frame strong.
Thin sheets of steel are laid on
top of the beams on each floor.
Wet concrete is poured over the
steel decking.
Cement workers have to level
the concrete quickly before it
hardens.
In a day, the floor is safe to
walk on.

Cranes are powerful machines that lift materials from the ground up to where they are needed. Truck cranes that move on wheels are used at the start of construction. Then tower cranes do the lifting to higher floors. Tower cranes rise hundreds of feet into the air and can reach out just as far.

People called ironworkers climb all
over the framework of a skyscraper
as if they are on a giant jungle gym.
The workers walk along the narrow
beams without fear of falling.
They fit beams and girders to
the columns and bolt or weld them
together.
These joints have to be just as strong as
the beams and columns are themselves.

Many skyscrapers are built with
steel beams and columns.
Other skyscrapers are built with
concrete beams and columns
reinforced with steel rods.
Beams and columns are made in
different shapes.
Columns have a ⲓ shape
to help keep them from bending.
Beams have a I shape that allows
them to carry heavy weights.

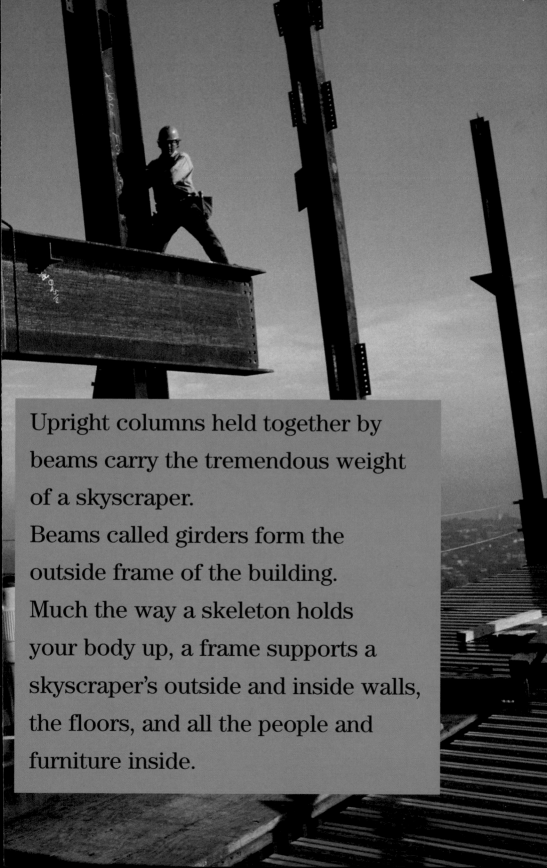

Upright columns held together by
beams carry the tremendous weight
of a skyscraper.
Beams called girders form the
outside frame of the building.
Much the way a skeleton holds
your body up, a frame supports a
skyscraper's outside and inside walls,
the floors, and all the people and
furniture inside.

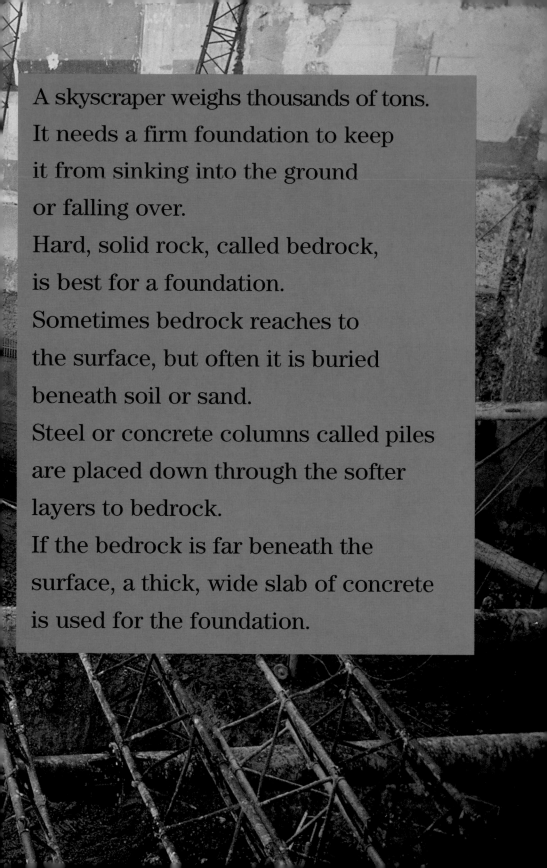

A skyscraper weighs thousands of tons.
It needs a firm foundation to keep
it from sinking into the ground
or falling over.
Hard, solid rock, called bedrock,
is best for a foundation.
Sometimes bedrock reaches to
the surface, but often it is buried
beneath soil or sand.
Steel or concrete columns called piles
are placed down through the softer
layers to bedrock.
If the bedrock is far beneath the
surface, a thick, wide slab of concrete
is used for the foundation.

The Empire State Building, in
New York City, was completed
in 1931.
It has a steel frame, concrete
floors, and outside walls of
brick and stone.
This 102-story building was
the tallest in the world for
40 years.
It has more than 1,800 steps to
the top.
It would take most people more
than an hour to climb that high.
But high-speed elevators take
you to the top in just a minute.

The first modern skyscraper
was built in Chicago in 1885.
Soon, many cities began to
build skyscrapers.
These created a lot more
space for people to work and
live in the downtown areas.

The steel frame of the Reliance Building in Chicago
was put together in only four weeks.

Today's skyscrapers would not be possible without a strong metal frame.

Early buildings could only be 50 or 60 feet high because the brick and stone walls had to be very thick to support the heavy weight of the floors above.

Steel is so strong that a thin cable can lift a cement truck. And steel frames make it possible to build skyscrapers as tall as you want.

Steel is made by heating iron ore and small amounts of coal and other substances in a large blast furnace.

This early skyscraper was built in Italy
more than 650 years ago.
It was built on soft ground.
Over the years it began to tilt to
one side.
We call it the Leaning Tower of Pisa.
We now know that skyscrapers need
a firm foundation to keep them
from sinking.